NUMBER 457

THE ENGLISH EXPERIENCE

ITS RECORD IN EARLY PRINTED BOOKS
PUBLISHED IN FACSIMILE

The publishers acknowledge their gratitude to
the Curators of the Bodleian Library, Oxford
for their permission to reproduce
the Library's copy, Shelfmark:8°.L.78 Th (3).

Library of Congress Catalog Card Number:
70-38186

S.T.C.No. 11162

Collation: A^6, B-F^{12}, G^6

Published in 1972 by

Theatrvm Orbis Terrarvm Ltd.,
O.Z.Voorburgwal 85, Amsterdam

&

Da Capo Press Inc.
-a subsidiary of Plenum Publishing Corporation-
277 West 17th Street, New York N.Y. 10011

Printed in the Netherlands
ISBN 90 221 0457 5

A LINE

OF LIFE.

Pointing at the *Immortalitie* of a Vertuous
N A M E.

Printed by *W. S.* for *N. Butter*, and
are to be sold at his shop neere
Saint *Austens* gate.
1 6 2 0.

WISE,
and therein
NOBLE.

Ambition bee-
ing *sooner dis-*
couered by a-
cting then plot-
ting, *can rarely perso-*
nate practise in studie,
vnlesse the Arts them-
selues, *which in them-*
selues are liberall, *should*
be too curiously censured,
too inquisitiuely confi-
ned.

ned. It is an easie vani-
ty, in these dayes of libertie, to be a conceited In-
terpreter, but a difficult
commendation to bee
a serious Author : for
whatsoever is at all times
honestly intended, often-
times is too largely con-
strued. Generall collections meet (not seldome)
with particular applica-
tions, and those so dan-
gerous, that it is more
safe, more wise, to pro-
fesse a free silence, then a
necessarie industrie.
Here in this (scarce an)
handfull of discourse, is
deciphered, not what any
perso-

personally is, but what a-
ny personally may be : to
the intent, that by the
view of others wounds,
we might prouide play-
sters and cures for our
owne, if occasion impose
them. It is true, that all
men are not borne in one,
the same, or the like pu-
ritie of qualitie or con-
dition; for in some, Cu-
stome is so become ano-
ther Nature, that Rea-
son, is not the mistresse,
but the seruant, not the
directresse but the foyle
to their passions. Folly is
a sale-able merchandise,
whose factour, youth is

A 3   *not*

not so allowedly profest in young men, as pleasure in men of any age : yet are the ruines, the calamities, the wofull experiences of sundrie presidents and samplars of indiscretion and weakenesse (even in noted, and sometimes in great ones) so apparent, so daily, that no Antidote against the infection, disease, leprosie of so increasing an evill, can be reputed superfluous. For my part, I ingeniously acknowledge, that hitherto (how euer the course hath proued a barre to my thrift, yet) I

neuer

neuer fawned vpon any mans *Fortunes*, whose person and merit I preferred not. Neither hath any court-ship of applause, set me in a higher straine, a higher pinnacle of opinion, then seuerest *Approbation* might make warrantable. Howbeit euen in these few lines that follow, my ayme hath not beene so grossely leuelled, that I meant to chuse euery Reader for my Patron: considering that none can challenge any interest herein from me (vnlesse he challenge it

A 4   by

by way of an *usurped impropriation*) whom I my selfe doe not out of some certaine knowledge and allowance of Desert, as it were poynt out and at, with my finger, and confesse that Hic est, *it is this one and onely.* By which marke, I can deny no man (not guiltie to himselfe of a selfe-unworthinesse) to call it his owne : at least, none of those, who freely returne the defects to their proper owner, and the benefit (if any may be) of this little worke to their own use and themselues. So much

much it is to bee pre*su*med, the *verie taliarie*
Law may require and
obtaine. In all things, no
one thing can more re-
qui*s*itely bee ob*s*erued to
be pra*ct*i*s*ed, *then* The
Golden Meane : *The
exemplification where-
of, howeuer heretofore*
*attributed, I dare not *s*o
poorely *v*nder-value my
*s*elfe and labours, as not
to call mine. But if I
*should farther exceede,
I might exceede that
meane, which I haue en-
deuoured to commend.
Let him that is wife, and
therein noble , a*ssume*
                        pro-

*properly to himselfe this
interest, that I cannot
distrust the successefull
acceptation, where the
sacrifice is a thriftie
loue; the Patron a great
man good (for to be tru-
ly good is to be great)
And the Presentor, a
feodarie to such as are
maisters not more of
their own Fortunes then
their owne affections.*

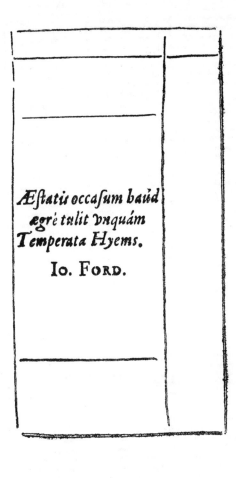

Æstatis occasum haud
ægrè tulit vnquám
Temperata Hyems.

Io. Ford.

LINEA
VITÆ:

A Line of Life.

TO liue , and
to liue well ,
are diſtinct in
theſelues , ſo
peculiarly as is the Ac-
TOR and the ACTION.
All men couet the for-
mer, as if it were the to-

B   tall

tall and fouereigne felicitie of a humane condition : And fome few purfue the latter, becaufe it giues an eternity to their bleffedneffe. The difference between thofe two is, *Life* defired for the only benefit of liuing, feares to dye; for fuch men that fo liue, when they dye, both dye finally & dye all : But a *good Life* aymes at another mark; for fuch men as indeauour to liue well, liue with an expectation of death, and they when they dye, dye to liue, and

and liue for euer. In this
respect hath death (be-
ing the parting of a pre-
cious Ghest from a rui-
nous Inne , the soule
from the bodie) beene
by the Ancients, styled
a Hauen of safetie, a fi
nishing of Pilgrimages,
a resting from trauaile,
a passage to glorie. Eue-
rie man that most shuns
it (and he most shunnes
it that most feares it)
runnes notwithstanding
wilfully to meet it, euen
then posting to it, when
hee abhorres it: for (the
comparison is liuely &
remarkeable)as he who

in a Shippe, directs his
courſe to ſome Port;
whether he ſtand, walk,
reuell, ſleepe, lie downe,
or any way elſe diſpoſe
himſelſ, is notwithſtan-
ding alwaies driuen on
to the period of his voy-
age : So in this Ship of
our mortalitie, howſoe-
uer wee limit our cour-
ſes, or are ſuited in any
fortune of proſperitie or
lowneſſe, in this great
Sea of the World; yet
by the violence and per-
petuall motion of time,
are we compeld to pace
onward to the laſt and
long   home   of   our
graues,

graues, and then the vi-
ctorie of Life is conclu-
ded in the victory of our
ends.

It is granted in *Philo-
sophie*, that *Action* is
the Crowne of Vertue.
It cannot in *reason* (the
light of Philosophie) be
denied, that *perseuerance*
is the Crowne of Acti-
on: and then *Diuinitie*
the Queene of Nature
will confirme, that *suffe-
rance* is the Crowne of
perseuerance. For to be
vertuous without the
testimonie of imploy-
ment, is as a rich Mine-
rall in the heart of the
B 3   Earth,

Arist. in 1.
*Ethic. l.
Cicer. in off.*

Earth, vn-vſeful becauſe
vnknowne ; yet to bee
vertuouſly imployed,
and not to continue, is
like a ſwiſt runner for a
Prize, who can with eaſe
gaine it from others, but
ſlothfully ſitteth downe
in the middle way ; but
to perſeuere in well-do-
ing without a ſence of a
dutie, only with hope of
reward, is like an Indi-
an Dromedarie, that
gallops to his common
Inne, prickt on-wardes
with the deſire of Pro-
uender. *It is beaſt-like*
not to differ from beaſts,
aſwell in the abuſe of rea-
ſon,

son, as it would bee in the defect.

ACTION, PERSEVERANCE IN ACTION, SVFFERANCE IN PERSEVERANCE, are the three golden linkes that furnish vp the richeſt Chain wherwith a good man can bee adorned; They are a tripartite counterpawne, wherby wee hold the poſſeſſion of life, whoſe Charter or Poll Deed (as they terme it) are youth till twentie, manhood till fortie, olde age till our end. And hee who beginnes not in the ſpring

of his minoritie to bud
forth fruits of vertuous
hopes, or hopefull de-
ferts, which may ripen
in the Summer of con-
firmed manhood; rarely
or neuer yeelds the crop
of a plentifull memory
in his age, but preuents
the winter of his laft
houre, in the barren Au-
tume of his worft houre,
by making an euen rec-
koning with time mif-
fpent, dying without a-
ny *Iffue* to inherit his remembrance or commē-
dation.

    Heere is then a pre-
paration made to the
ground-

ground-worke & foundation wheron the structure and faire building of a minde nobly furnisht must stand: which for the perpetuitie and glorie of so lasting a monument, cannot altogether vnfitly bee applyed to a LINE OF LIFE. For whosoeuer shall leuell & square his whole course by this iust proportion, shall (as by a line) bee led not only to vnwinde himselfe from out the Labyrinth and Maze of this naturall & troublesome Race of frailtie, but to flie vp in

B 5   the

the middle path, the *via lactea* of immortalitie in his name on Earth, to the Throne of life, and perfection in his whole man, and to an immortalitie that cannot bee changed.

Deceiuing and deceiueable *Palmesters*, who will vndertake by the view of the hand, to bee as expert in foretelling the courſe of life to come to others, as they are ignorant of their own in themſelues, haue framed and found out three chiefe lines in the hand, wherby to diuine

future

future euents; *The line of life, The middle naturall line, and the table line.* According to the fresh colour or palenes, length or shortnesse, bredth or narrownesse, straitnesse or obliquitie, continuance or intermissiõ of either of these, they presume to censure the manners, the infirmities, the qualities, the verie power of Life or Death of the person. But the *line of life* is the eminent mark they must be directed by, to the perfection of their Master-piece. All which, are as far

far from truth as won-
der; onely it is true and
wonderfull, that any ig-
norance can be so delu-
ded. Another *line of life*
is the most certaine and
infallible rule , which
wee as we are men, and
more then men; Christi-
ans, & more then Chri-
stians, the image of our
maker; must take our le-
uel by. Neither is iudge-
ment to be giuen by the
ordinary lineaments of
the furniture of Nature,
but by the noble in-
dowments of the mind,
whose ornaments or
ruines are then most ap-
pa-

parently goodly or miserable, when as the actions we doe, are the euidences of a primitiue puritie; or a deriuatiue deprauation. Here is a great labour to indure, a great strength in that labour to conquer, a great Resolution in that strength to triumph, requisite, before wee can climbe the almost impregnable and inaccessible toppe of glorie; which they that haue attempted haue found, & they that haue found haue enioyed to their own happines and wonder

der of imitation.

RESOLVTION is the plotter and the Actor, nay, it is both the plot and the Act it selfe that must prompt vs how to doe, aswell as it must point vs out what to do before wee can as much as take into the hands of our purposed constancie, this *line* which must direct vs to life, & make vs to liue.

Whatsoeuer therefore in those briefe ensuing collections is inserted, to patterne and personate an excellent man, must be concluded and
vn-

vnderſtood for methods
ſake in this one only at-
tribute, RESOLVTION.
For by it are exempli-
fied the perfections of
the minde, conſiſting in
the whole furniture of
an enriched ſoule; and
to it are referred the no-
bleſt actions, which are
the externall arguments
and proofes of the trea-
ſure within: For as it is a
State Maxime in Poli-
cie, that *Force abroad in
Warre is of no force, but
rather Raſhneſſe then
Souldierie, vnleſſe there
bee counſell peaceably at
home to direct for expe-*
di

dition: so are all actions
of Resolution in the
Oeconomie and house-
hold gouernment of a
mans owne particular
priuate wealth, but shi-
ningfollies, vnlesse there
bee a consultation first
held within him for de-
termining the commo-
ditie, the conueniencie
and commendation of
such actions , aswell in
doing, as when they are
done.

Order in euerie taske
is for conceipt easiest,
for demonstration playn-
nest, for Imitation su-
rest. Let vs then take
into

into our confideration
this *Line of Life*, and
trace the way wherein
wee are to trauaile, kee-
ping our eye on the
Compaffe whereby we
may runne to the Para-
dife of memorable hap-
pineffe. And firft it is to
be obferued, That *Refo-
lution* hath three bran-
ches; The one concerns
a mans owne particular
perfon for the carriage
of himfelfe in his proper
dutie, and fuch an one is
knowne by none other
note, then in beeing A
M A N : Another con-
cernes a mans imploy-
ment

ment in affaires for his
Countrey, Prince, and
Common-wealth, and
such a one as is knowne
by the generall name of
A PVBLIKE MAN. The
last concernes a mans
voluntarie traffique in
ciuill causes without the
imposition of authori-
tie, only vrged on to
performe the offices of
a friend, as a priuate
Statist to seuerall ends,
all tending to goodnes
and vertue; and such a
one is euer to be call'd a
GOOD MAN. In euerie
one of those there is a
plentifull imployment

pre-

presenting it selfe to the liberall choyce for ennobling themselues with publique honors, or gayning them the truest honour *A deserued fame*, which is one (if worthie) of the best and highest rewards of vertue.

Superfluous it were and vnnecessarie, to enter into the contentious lists of diuided Philosophers, or vnreconciled Schoolemen, for the absolute and punctuall definition of man; Since, it sufficeth vs to be assured that he is

Of the first, a man.

is mainely and yet pi-
thily diftinguifh't from
all other created fub-
ftances in the only pof-
feffion of a *reafonable*
foule. This royall pre-
rogatiue alone poynts
him to be noblest of
creatures; and to fpeak
truth, in an affertion
not to be gain-faid, he
containes the fumma-
ry of all the *great world*,
in the *little world* of
himfelfe. As then the
Fabricke of the globe
of the earth would of
neceffitie runne to the
confufion out of which
it was firft refined, if
                    there

there were not a great
and watchfull proui-
dence, to meaſure it in
the iuſt ballance of pre-
ſeruing and ſuſtayning;
ſo conſequently, with-
out queſtion, the frame
of our humane compo-
ſition, muſt prepoſte-
rouſly ſinke vnder its
owne burthen, if warie
and prudent direction,
as well in manners as in
deedes, reſtraine it not
from the diſſolution
and wracke, the pro-
cliuitie of corrupted
Nature doth hourely
ſlide into.

*A mans minde is the
man*

*Cicero
Ariſt.*

man himſelfe (ſaid the Romane Orator) and the chiefeſt of the Grecian Naturaliſts , was confident to auerre, that *the temperature of the minde followed the temperature of the body.* It were a Leſſon worthie to bee cond, if eyther of thoſe rules may be poſitiuely receiued: For out of the firſt, as any man feeles his inclinations and affections, thereafter let him iudge himſelfe to bee ſuch a man. Out of the latter it may be gathered ; how eaſie it

were

were, for euerie man to be his owne Schoole-mafter, in the conformation or reformation of his life, without other tutour then himfelfe.

Socrates his fpeech of the vfe of mirrours or looking glaffes, concludes whatfoeuer can bee ranged in many wordes of this fubiect, and is therefore notorioufly vfefull, and vfefully notable; When thou viewest thy felfe in a mirrour, (faid that wife man) furueyeft thy complexion, thy propor-

portion, if thy face be
more faire, louely , and
sweeter then others,
thy bodie straighter,
thy lineaments perfe-
cter; cōsider how much
more thou art bound
by that, to match those
blessings of Nature,
with the accomplish-
ment of more noble
qualities, then others of
a courser mould. If on
the other side, thou per-
ceiue thy face defor-
med, thy body croo-
ked, thy outward con-
stitution vnsightly or
mishapen; by so much
the more hast thou rea-
son

son to liue a good life,
that thereby concord
of vertuous conditions,
may supply the defects
of Nature, and make
thee more beautifull in
wardly to the eye of
iudgement, then out-
wardly thou couldst
haue beene to the eyes
of popular delight.

In short, to be a *man*,
the first branch of reso-
lution is to know, feele,
and moderate affecti-
ons, which like traitors,
and disturbers of peace,
rise vp to alter & quite
change the Lawes of
reason, by working in

C the

the feeble, and often-
times the founder parts,
an innouation of folly.
Hee can seldome be a
flourishing member of
a bodie politique, and
so a *publique deseruing
man*; but more rarely,
scantly euer, a reconci-
ler of diuisions, and so
a ciuill *good man* for
others, that begins not
betimes to discharge his
owne dutie to himselfe.
The old Prouerbe was,
(and it is lamentable, to
speake with truth, and
say it is) that *A man
is a beast to a man*; but
it must be of necessitie
gran-

*Homo ho-
mini lupus.*

granted, when a man to himselfe is a *Monster*, or more prouerbially, *a Deuill*.

It is said of C AIVS CVRIO, that hee was a man most *wittily wicked*, and most *singularly eloquent* in mischiefe against the Common-wealth. What rarities were here lost? (like a Diamond set in a rushen ring:) How much better had it been for him, to haue had a *duller braine*, if better imployed, and a *flower tongue*, if auaileable for the publique good? E-
C 2   uery

Villeius Paterc. lib. 2.

uery man fhould in his
owne perfon, endeuour
and ftriue to be like *Ca-*
toes Orator, a goodman,
and expert in pleading,
Firft *good*, then *expert*;
For of fo much richer
price is *vertue* then
Art. *Art* without *ver-*
tue being like the *Can-*
tharides, whofe wings
puld off, they haue pret-
tie colours to pleafe the
eye, but poifonous fub-
ftances to be receiued
into the ftomack. How
eafie it is to guild a rot-
ten poft, to paint a Se-
pulcher, to varnifh an
ill meaning, is foone re-
foued

Fabius,
*orat.lib.*12.
cap. 1.

Plin. lib.
11.*cap.*35.

folued : Many men can *ſpeake well*, few men will *doe well* ; The reaſon, for that we couet to be thought what wee are not, and yet continue to be what wee are aſhamed to be thought.

The excellēcy of goodneſſe is apparent mainly in this one poynt, that euen thoſe who leaſt practiſe it in outward appearance, cunningly labour to make it the marke whereto all their actions (how foule ſoeuer in the iſſue) leuell at. It was truely obſerued by a

C 3　　　graue

graue Author, That
there was neuer any
publique mischiefe at-
tempted in a State by
euen Atheists, or very
incarnate Deuils, but
Religion was their co-
lour to effect it; at least
a shew of some false
zeale in as false a wor-
ship. For there must be
an intention of vertue
in the worst actions, o-
therwise they could ne-
uer haue passage by any
publique approbation;
Insomuch, that hypo-
crisie is reputed the su-
rest & the safest ground
of pollicie.

By

By this appeareth the
richneffe of vertue, that
euen fuch as moft op-
pofe it, muft and are
compelled to acknow-
ledge it for beft. In like
manner, euery man in
his particular to diftin-
guifh his actions, is in
his knowledge guiltie
and confcious of what
he doth or fhould doe.
We were not borne to
feed, fleepe, and fpinne
out our webbe of life in
the delicate foftneffe of
vanitie, or floath; wee
were not borne to tra-
fique in follies, and to
make merchandize of

our senfualities ; wee
were not borne to reuel
in the apifhneffe of ri-
diculous expence of
time ; wee were not
borne to be Panders to
to that great Whore of
a declyning Reafon ,
bewitching pleaſure :
we were not borne to
laugh at our owne fe-
curitie, but to bewayle
it ; we were not borne
to liue for our felues,
but to our felues; as we
were not on the other
fide borne to dye to
our felues, but for our
felues. We muft learne
to reioyce in true good-
neffe,

neſſe, not vain delights:
For as we cannot iudge
him to haue a light
heart alwaies, that ſom-
times laughes (for euen
in laughter there is a
ſadneſſe,) ſo wee muſt
not imitate by any out-
ward demeanor, to be-
wray the minoritie of
our Reſolution, except
we would be as childiſh
in vnderſtanding as in
action.

What infinite inti-
cers hath a man as he is
a meere man, to with-
draw him from an ere-
cted heart ? As the
temptation of a repu-

ted beautie, the inuite-
ment of a preſented
honour, the bewitch-
ing of an inforced
wealth , the Lethar-
gie and diſeaſe of an in-
fectious Court-grace ;
yet all and euerie one
of theſe (with what o-
ther appendances ſo-
euer belonging vnto
them) are (if not wiſe-
ly made vſe of) but glo-
rious ſnares, dangerous
baites, golden poyſons,
dreaming diſtructions,
ſnares to intrappe the
mightineſſe of conſtan-
cie ; Baites to deceiue
the conſtancie of man-
hood,

hood, poyfons to cor-
rupt the manhood of
Refolution; deftruction
to quite caft away the
Refolution of a iuft de-
fert.

Now for a mans car-
riage in his particular
dutie, what can hee de-
termine of, fince he hath
not more himfelfe, and
his own affections to af-
fault and batter his Re-
folution in the path of
Vertue, then a world of
prefidents, of partners,
of helpers, to perfwade
and draw him on to the
full meafure of an vn-
worthy life. It is a la-
bor

bor wel worthy a Chronicle (and chronicled will bee in a perpetuall memorie) to withstand the seuere assault of Folly, pressing on with so infinite an Armie of followers and admirers as shee is accompanyed with : what can one *priuate man* do against such a multitude of temptations ? Either hee must consent to doe as they doe; or dissent and hate them : if consent, hee is mischieuous with many; if dissent, vertuous by himselfe; and the last is without controuersie

the

the best. Since neuer to
haue seene euill is no
praise to well doing; but
where the Actours of
Mischiefe are a Nation,
there and amongst them
to liue well is a Crowne
of immortall commen-
dation.

A Golden Axiome
there was registred a-
mongst the Ciuilians in
the daies of *Iustinian:*
That it was not conueni-
ent for any man to pry
and looke after what was
done at Rome, but to ex-
amine iustly what ought
there to bee done. Rome
was then the Mart of
the

the World, all forts of
euery people came thi-
ther, from thence to re-
ceiue the Oracles of life
(as they might bee ter-
med:) yet doth it not follow that any one man
with the multitude,
fhould runne to *Rome*,
to fucke the infection of
diffolute intemperature.
Vanity moft commonly
rides coach't in the high
way, the beaten way, the
common way; But *Ver-*
tue and Moderation
walkes alone. It may be
faid, what profit can re-
dound, what commen-
dation, what reward, for
one

one man to bee singular
against many ? O the
profit is infinite , the
commendation memo-
rable , the reward im-
mortall. It is true the
olde Greeke Prouerbe
concluded, that *one man
was no man*; yet with
their most approoued
Authours, by the verie
word MANY , were the
worst sort of people vn-
derstood, and by FEW
the best. For certaine-
ly there is not any al-
lurement could lull men
in the mist of their mis-
deeds, so much as those
two pestilent yoke-fel-
lowes

lowes and twinnes of confusion, *The multitude of offenders, and the libertie of offending.* They are both Examples and Schoolemasters, to teach euen the very ignorant (whose simplicitie else might be their excuse) to do what (if others did not) they might accidentally slide into, but not so eagerly pursue.

To conclude this point, it may somewhat too truly be said, though not by way of discouragement, yet of caueat, what by the procliuitie and

and proneneſſe of our
frailtie is warrantable;
Let no man bee too confi-
dent of his owne merit,
The beſt doe erre : Let no
man relye too much on
his owne Iudgement, the
wiſeſt are deceiued : yet
let euery man ſo con-
ceiue of himſelfe , that
he may indeuour to bee
ſuch a one , as diſtruſt
ſhal not make him care-
leſſe , or confidence ſe-
cure.

It followes that the
very conſideration of
being men, ſhould ſom-
what rectifie our croo-
ked inclinations , and
en-

ennoble our actions to
keepe vs worthy of the
priuiledge wee haue a-
boue beasts : otherwise
only to be a man in sub-
stance and name, is no
more glorie then to bee
knowne and distingui-
shed from a very beast
in nature.

Presidents from An-
tiquitie may plentifully
be borrowed, to set be-
fore vs what some men
haue beene, not as they
were Commanders, or
employed for the Com-
monwealth; but as they
were Commanders of
their owne infirmities,
and

and employed for the
Commonwealth of their
own particular persons.
Epaminondas amongst
the *Thebanes*, is worthy
of note and memorie e-
uen to our Ages, and
those that shall succeed
vs; Hee (as the Philoso-
pher recordeth) chose
rather to bee moderate
alone, then madde with
the multitude; chusing
at all times to consult
with himselfe in excel-
lent things, not with his
Countreymen to giue
Lust, Dalliance, Effemi-
nate softnes a Regiment
in the Kingdome of his
thoughts;

*Plutarch. in
Apotheg.*

*Cicero de
leg.lib.*3.

*Iuuenal.
Sat.*14.

*Epiſt.*98.

thoughts; no not of his thoughts, much leſſe of his Actions. *Phocion* among the *Athenians*, *Brutus* among the *Romanes*, are for their particular cariage of themſelues as they were only men, well worthy of all remembrance: And the ſententious *Seneca* is bold to ſay, that all Ages will euer hatch and bring forth many ſuch as *Clodius*, (a man bent to miſchiefe) but rarely any Age another *Cato*, a man ſo ſincere, ſo free from corruption, and ſo ſeuere a Cenſurer of himſelfe.   But

But what need we to ſearch hiſtories of other times, or the deſerts of another Nation, when in our owne Land, in our owne dayes, wee might eaſily patterne what a man ſhould bee or not bee, by what others haue bin? Among many, two of late times are iuſtly examined; not as they were different in fortune, in yeares, in degree, but as they differed in the vſe of the gifts of their mind. The firſt was IOHN, the laſt and yongeſt Lord HAR-RINGTON, whoſe rare and

and admirable courſe of
life(not as he was a No-
ble man,for then indeed
it were miraculous, but
as a man,) deſerues all
prayſe and imitation
from all. Of whome it
may without flatterie
(for what benefit can
accrue to flatter the
dead?) or affection bee
ſaid, That He amongſt
a World of men attay-
ned euen in his youth,
not only to grauitie in
his behauiour, to wiſe-
dome in his vnderſtan-
ding, to ripeneſſe in his
carriage,to diſcretion in
his diſcourſe,but to per-
feċtion

fection in his action : A man wel-deferuing euen the teftimonie of a religious learned Diuine.

But for that his owne merit is his beft commendation, and queftionleffe his fureft reward for morall gifts: let him reft in his peace whileft the next is to bee obferued.

SIR WALTIR RAVLEIGH may be a fecond Prefident, a mã known, and wel-deferuing to be knowne; A man endued not with common endowments being ftored with the beft of Natures fur-

furniture, taught much by much experience, experienc'd in both fortunes so feelingly and apparently, that it may tru'y bee controuerted whether hee were more happie or miferable; yet beholde in him the ftrange Character of a *meere man*, a man fubiect to as many changes of *refolution*, as *refolute* to bee the inftrument of change: *Politique*, and yet in *Policie* fo vnfteddie, that his too much apprehenfion was the foile of his iudgement. *For what man foeuer*

leanes

leanes too credulously to his owne strength, not supported by the firme Pillars of *Constancy* and *Vertue*, that man cannot choose but fall vnder the weight of his owne burthen: And so did he, being faulty in nothing more, then not applying himselfe to the trust of such friends as laboured to doe him seruice, in honest and honourable Designes. In a word, his *Wisdome* and *Courage* appeared (late enough, though not too late) in his last demeanour; for that *not making*

D

king himselfe leſſe when he was great, he ſtroue to be ſo great in his reſolution when he came to bee nothing, I ſpeake of his end, at his end. So heere may this point bee fitly cloſed vp, that a mans particular carriage in his proper dutie, is a ſweet and readie preparation for enabling him to vndergoe the ſecond branch of a noble Reſolution in publique imployment, by beeing made for his Prince and Countrey A PVBLIKE MAN: which to doe, theſe few lines comprehend

hend all what the for-
mer Discourse hath am-
plified; Namely that *the
only felicitie of a good
life, depends in doing all
things freely, by beeing
content with what wee
haue (for wee speake of a
morall man.) This is to
remember that we are
mortall, that our dayes
passe on, and our life
slides away without re-
couerie.*

*Senea E-
pist.*128.

   Great is the taske, the
labour painfull, the dis-
charge full of danger, &
the dagers full of Enuy,
that he must of necessi-
tie vndergoe, that like a

Of the
second
branch,
A Pub-
like man.

D 2   blaze

blaze vpon a Mountain,
stands neerest in grace
to his Prince : or like a
vigilant Sentinell in a
Watch-tower , busies
and weakens his owne
naturall and vitall spi-
rits, to administer Equa-
litie and Iustice to all,
according to the requi-
sition of his office.

It is lamentable and
much to bee pittyed,
when places of Autho-
rity in a Cōmonwealth,
are disposed of to some,
whose vnworthinesse or
disabilitie brings a scan-
dall, a scorne, and a re-
proch to both the place
and

and the Minister.

The best Law-makers amongst the Ancients, were so curious in their choice of men in Office in the Commonwealth, that precisely and peremptorily, they reputed that STATE plagued, whipped, tormented, wounded, yea wounded to death, where the subordinate Gouernours were not aswell vnblemished in their liues and actions, as in their names and reputation.

A PVBLIKE MAN hath not more neede to be *Bonus Ciuis*, a good

Plato 3.6. *& 12.de leg.& 7.de Repub. Arist. 5.& 6.Poit. Isocrat. in Pan.*

D 3   Sta-

Statist, then *Bonus Vir,*
good in himselfe; a very
faire and large *Line* is
limmed out to square
by it, a direct path that
leades to a vertuous
Name, if a man acquite
himselfe nobly, iustly,
and wisely, in well stee-
ring the Helme of State
that he sits at; otherwise
his Honours are a bur-
then, his Height a Curse;
his Fauours a Destructi-
on, his Life a Death, and
his Death a Misery: A
Misery in respect of his
after Defamation, as-
well as of his after ac-
compt.

Far

Far from the present
purpose it is to diue in-
to the depth of *Policie*,
or to set downe any po-
sitiue rules, what a right
Statesman should be; for
that were with *Phormio*
the Philosopher to read
a Lecture of Souldierie
to *Hannibal* the most
cunningest Warriour of
his time; & consequent-
ly as *Phormio* was by
Hannibal to be iustly
laughed at , so aswell
might *Seneca* haue writ-
ten to *Nero* the Art of
Crueltie ; or *Cicero* to
his brother *Quintus* the
Commendation of An-
D 4   ger.

ger. The summe of these
briefe Collections, is intended to recreate the
minde, not to informe
Knowledge in practice;
but to conforme Prac-
tice to Knowledge :
Whereto no indeauor
can bee found more re-
quisite, more auaileable,
then an vndeceiuing les-
son of an impartiall ob-
seruation; wherin if our
studies erre not with
many and those most
approued, thus we haue
obserued.

First , of publique
men there are two ge-
nerall sorts; The one,
                    such

Two sorts
of publike
men.

such as by the speciall
fauour of their Prince
(which fauour cannot
ordinarily be conferred
without some mayne
and euident note of de-
sert) haue beene raised,
to a supereminent ranck
of honour, and so by
degrees (as it for the
most part alwayes hap-
pens) to speciall places
of weightie imploy
ment in the common
wealth. *The other* sort
are such as the Prince
according to his iudge-
ment, hath out of their
owne sufficiencie, ad-
uaunced to particular

D 5 offi-

offices, whether for administration of iustice, for execution of Law, for necellitie of seruice, and the like, being according to their education and studie, enabled for the discharge of those places of authoritie; and *these two* are the onely chiefe and principall members of imploiment, vnder that head of whose politike bodie they are the most vsefull & stirring members.

Against both those publique persons, there are *two capitall and*

dead-

deadly opposites (if it
were poſſible) to be-
charme their reſoluti-
ons , and blot out their
name from the L I N E
O F L I F E , by which
they ſhould bee led to
the endleſſe immorta-
litie of an immortalitie,
in an euer-flouriſhing
commendation . *The
first* are poyſoners of
vertue, the betrayers of
goodneſſe , the bloud-
ſuckers of innocencie :
The latter , the cloſe
deathſ-men of merit,
the plotters againſt ho-
neſtie, and the executi-
oners of honors ; They
are

are in two words disco-
uered, *Blandientes &*
Sæuientes, Flatterers,
and priuie Murtherers.
It is a disputable questi-
on, and well worthie a
canuase and discussion
in the schools, to decide
which of the two doe
the greatest iniurie to
noble personages. How
be it most apparent it
is, that enuie, the inse-
parable companiō that
accompanies the vertu-
ous, doeth not worke
more mischiefe for the
finall ouerthrow of a
noble and deseruing
man, thē Flattery doth,
for

for driuing that noble
and deſeruing man into
the ſnares of enuie. No
man can be, or ſhould
be reputed a God; and
then how eaſie it is for
any man of the choy-
ceſt temper, of the ſoun-
deſt apprehenſion, of
the gracefulleſt educa-
tion, of the ſincereſt au-
ſteritie of life; how ea-
ſie it is for him to fall
into many errours, into
many vnbecomming
follies, into many paſſi-
ons, and affections: his
onely being *a man* is
both ſufficient proofe,
and yet ſufficient ex-
cuſe.

cuſe. The eloquenteſt and graueſt Diuine of all the Ancients, confeſt out of his owne experience, *Non eſt mihi vicinior hoſtis memet ipſo :* that he had not a more neere enemie to him then himſelfe. For he that hath about him his frailtie to corrupt him, a World to beſot him, an aduerſarie to terrifie him ; and laſtly, a death to deuoure him : how ſhould hee but bee inueigled with the inticements of the *two firſt,* and ſo conſequently conſent to the vnſteadineſſe

nesse of his temptation
before he be drawne to
a serious consideration
of the danger of the *two
last?* Especially as wee
are men, being not one-
ly subiect to the lapses
and vanities of men, but
as we are eminent men,
in grace and fauour, in
prioritie of titles, of
place, & of command;
hauing men to sooth vs
vp in the maintenance
and countenancing of
those euils, which else
doubtlesse, could not at
one time or other, but
appeare before vs in
their own vglinesse and
deformitie.   A

A Flatterer is the onely peſtilent bawd to great mens ſhames; the nurſe to their wantonneſſe; the fuell to their luſts; and with his poyſon of artificiall villanie, moſt times doth ſet an edge vnto their ryot, which otherwiſe would be blunted and rebated in the deteſtation of their owne violent poſting to a violent confuſion. Not vnwiſely did a wiſe man compare a *flattering Language to a ſilken halter,* which is *ſoft* becauſe *ſilken*, but *ſtrangling* be-

Diog. Laert. in vita Diog.

becaufe a *halter*. The words wherewith thofe *Panders of Vice* doe perfwade, are not fo louely, as the matters they dawbe ouer with their adulations, are abhominable. That is a bitter fweetneffe which is onely delicious to the pallate, and to the ftomacke deadly. It is reported, that all beafts are wonderfully delighted with the fent of the breath of the Panther, a beaft fierce and cruell by nature; but that they are elfe afrighted with the fterneneffe of his

Plin. hift. lib. 8. cap. 17.

his lookes: For which
cauſe , the Panther
when he hunts his prey,
hiding his grimme vi-
ſage, with the ſweet-
neſſe of his breath , al-
lures the other beaſtes
vnto him , who being
come within his reach,
hee rends and cruelly
doth dilaniate them.
Euen ſo, thoſe Patrons
and *minions of falſe*
pleaſures, *the Flatterers*
that they may prey vp-
on the credulitie of the
abuſed GREAT ONES,
imitate the Panthers,
extenuating , and as
much as in them lyes,
hi-

hiding the groffeneffe,
the vglineffe, the defor-
mitie of thofe follyes
they perfwade vnto;
and with a falfe gloffe,
varnifhing and fetting
out the Paradife of vn-
controlled pleafures, to
the ruine oft times of
the informed, and glo-
rie of their owne im-
pietie.

Is fuch a MIGHTIE
MAN inticed to ouer-
rule his Reafon, nay o-
uer-beare it, by giuing
fcope to his licentious
eye, firft to fee, then to
delight in, laftly, to couet a chafte beauty? A-
laffe,

lasse, how many swarms
of dependants, being
creatures to his great-
nesse, will not onely tell
him, mocke him, and
harden him in a readie
and pregnant deceipt,
that loue is courtly, and
women were in their
creation ordained to be
wooed, and to be won;
but also what numbers
of them, will thrust
themselues into imploi-
ment and seruile action,
to effect the lewdnesse
of desire, to corrupt
with promises, with
guifts, with perswasi-
ons, with threatnings,
with

with intreaties, to force
a Rape on Vertue, and
adulterate the chaste
bosome of spotlesse
simplicitie? A folly is
commited, how sleight
are they ready to proue
it , how sedulous to
sleighten , how dam
nably disposed to make
it nothing? Insomuch
as those vipers of hu-
manitie, are fitly to be
termed, the *mans whore*,
and the *womans knaue.*
Is such a mightie one
affected to such a suite,
as the graunt and pos-
session of it will draw a
curse vpon his head by
a ge-

a generall voyce, of a
generall fmart and de-
triment to the Com-
monwealth? How fud-
denly will thofe wilde
beafts, labour to affure
him, that the multi-
tudes loue is wonne by
keeping them in awe;
not by giuing way to
their giddineffe by any
affabilitie? Will another
aduaunce an vnworthy
Court-Ape, and op-
preffe a defertfull hope?
It were too tedious to
recite, what inceffant
approbations will bée
repeated by thefe *An-
thropophagi*, Thofe
men-

men-eaters, to make a
golden calfe an Idoll,
and a *neglected merite*
a laughter ? That such
a kinde of monſters,
may appeare in their
likeneſſe, as monſtrous
as in effect they are; It
is worthie obſeruation,
to ſee how when any
man, who whiles hee
ſtood chiefe in the
Princes fauour, they ho-
noured as an earthly
God, yet being decly-
ned from his Princes e-
ſtimation, it is worthie
to be noted, how ſpee-
dily, how ſwiftly, how
maliciouſly thoſe can-
kers

kers of a State will not
onely fall off, will not
onely difpife, will not
onely deride, but alfo
oppofe themfelues a-
gainft the partie difta-
fted.

As many fubtill pra-
ctizers of in'amie, haue
other fubordinate mi-
nifters of publique of-
fice and imployment in
a Common-wealth, to
betray them to their
ruine; yet euer and a-
non, they like inchan-
ted glaffes, fet them on
fire with the falfe light
of concealement and
extenuation. Let it be
fpo-

spoken with some au-
thority, borrowed from
experience of the elder
times, that men in high
places, are like some
hopelesse marriners, set
to sea in a leaking ves-
sel: there is no safetie,
no securitie, no com-
fort, no content in
greatnesse, vnlesse it be
most constantly armed
in the defensiue armor
of a selfe-worthie reso-
lution; especially when
their places they hold,
are hourely subiect to
innouation, as their
names (if they preuent
not their dangers by

E   lea

leauing them, and their liues at once) are to reproach, and the libertie of malice.

Flatterie to either publique perſons , is not more inductious on the one ſide, then enuie on the other is vigilant. Great men are by great men (not good men by good men) narrowly ſifted; their liues, their actions, their demeanors examined ; for that their places and honours are hunted after, as the *Beazar* for his preſeruatiues ; And then the leaſt blemiſh, the

the least slide, the least
error, the least offence,
is exasperated, made
capitall; the dangers en-
suing euer prooue (like
the wound of an ene-
mies sword) mortall,
and many times dead-
ly. Now in this case,
when the eye of iudge-
ment is awakened, *Flat-*
terie is discouered to
be but an Inmate to
Enuie; an Inmate, at
least, consulting toge-
ther though not dwel-
ling together, the one,
being Catarer to the
others bloudie ban-
quet; And some wise

E 2　　men

men haue been perſwaded, that the peſtilence, the rigour of Law, Famine, Sicknes, or War, haue not deuour'd more great ones then *Flattery and Enuie.*

Much amiſſe, & from the purpoſe it cannot bee, to giue inſtance in three publike Preſidents, of three famous Nations; all chancing within the compaſſe of twentie yeares. In *England* not long agoe, a man ſupereminent in Honours, deſertfull in many Seruices, indeared to a vertuous and

a

a wife Queene, ELIZA-
BETH *of glorious me-*
morie, and eternall hap-
pineſſe: A man too pub-
likely beloued, and too
confident of the loue he
held, ROBERT EARLE
OF ESSEX, and Earle
Marſhall of the King-
dome ; He, euen he that
was thought too high
to fall, and too fixed to
bee remoued; in a verie
handfull of time, felt the
miſery of Greatneſſe, by
relying on ſuch as flat-
tered and enuyed his
Greatneſſe. His end was
their end, and the exe-
cution of Law, is a wit-
E 3   neſſe

neſſe in him to Poſteri-
tie, how a publike per-
ſon is not at any time
longer happie, then hee
preſerues his happineſſe
with a Reſolution that
depends vpon the guard
of innocēcie & goodnes.

CHARLES DVKE OF
BYRON in *France*, not
long after him, ranne the
ſame Fate ; A Prince
that was reputed the in-
uincible Fortreſſe to his
King & Countrey: great
in deſert, and too great
in his Greatneſſe ; not
managing the fiery cha-
riot of his guiding the
Sunne of that Climate
with

with moderation; gaue teſtimonie by an impoſed and inexpected end, how a publike man in Authoritie, ſits but in Commiſſion on his own Delinquencie, longer then *Reſolution* in noble actions leuels at the immortalitie of *A Line of life*.

Laſtly, SIR IOHN VANOLDEN BARNE-VELT in the *Nether lands*, (whoſe aſhes are ſcarce yet colde) is and will bee a liuely preſident of the mutabilitie of Greatneſſe. Hee was the only one that traf-

E 4   fiqued

fiqued in the Coūfels of
forreine Princes, had fa-
ctors in all Courts , In-
telligencers amongst all
Chriftian nations;ftood
as the ORACLE of
the Prouinces, and was
euen the Moderator of
Policies of all forts:
was reputed to bee fe-
cond to none on Earth
for foundneffe of De-
fignes; was indeed his
Countreyes both My-
nion,Mirror,and Won-
der; yet enforcing his
publike Authoritie,too
much to bee feruant to
his priuate Ambition;
hee left the Tongue of
Iuftice

Iustice to proclayme
that *long life*, and a
peacefull death are not
granted or held by the
Charter of Honours,
except vertuous RESO-
LVTION renew the Pa-
tent, at a daily expence
of proficiencie in good-
neſſe.

Others freſh in me-
morie might bee inser-
ted, but theſe are yet
bleeding in the wounds
which they haue giuen
themſelues, and ſome
now liuing to this day,
who both haue had, and
doe enioy as great Ho-
nours, and are therefore

E 5   as

as incident to as many wofull changes, but that they wisely prouide to proppe their greatnesse with many greater deserts.

Here is in Text Letters layd before vs, the hazard, perill and casualty of A PVBLIKE MAN : the possibilitie what Miserie, Calamity, Ruine, Greatnesse and Popularitie may winde him into. Heere is decyphered the vnauoydable and incessant Persecutors of their Honors and Ioyes : *Flatterie and Enuie two ancient Cour-*

Courtiers. It comes now to conclusion, that it cannot be denyed, but those *publike men* haue (notwithstanding these) chiefe and immediate meanes in their owne powers, if they well and nobly order their cour-ses to make their Coun-trey their Debtors, and to enroll their names in the glorious Register of an euer-memorable Glorie: especially if they be not too partially do-ting on euery commen-dable Vertue, which in priuate men is reputed as it is, a Vertue; but in them

them a Miracle. Certainly (without disparagement to desert in great men) there are many particular persons, fit for publike imployments, whose ablenesse and sufficiencie , is no way inferiour to the prayses of the mightiest, but that they are clouded in their lownesse, & obscured in their priuatnesse, but else would & could giue testimony to the World, that all fulnesse and perfection is not confined to Eminence and Authoritie.

A Publike Man, there-

therefore, shunning the
Adulation of a Parasite
(which hee may easily
discouer, if hee wisely
examine his merit with
their Hyperbolical insi-
nuations,) then keeping
an euen course in the
processe of lawfull and
iust actions, auoyding
the toyles, snares and
trappes of the enuious,
cannot chuse in his own
life time, but build a monument, to which the
Triumph and Trophies
of his memorie, shall
giue a longer life then
the perpetuitie of stone,
Marble or Brasse can
pre-

preferue. Otherwife if
they ftand not on the
guard of their owne
Pietie and Wifedome,
they will vpon trifles
fometime or other bee
quarrelled againft and
euicted. Neyther may
they imagine that any
one taint (howfoeuer
they would bee conten-
ted to winke at it in
themfelues, fuppofing
it to be (as perhaps it is)
little, and not worthy re-
prehenfion) can efcape
vnefpyed. For the Mo-
rall of the Poets Ficti-
on is a goodly Leffon
for their inftruction. It
is

is said that *Thetis* the Mother of *Achilles*, drencht him being an Infant in the *Stygian* Waters, that thereby, his whole bodie might bee made invulnerable: but see the seueritie of Fate, for euen in that part of the heele that his Mother held him by, was hee shot by the Arrow of *Paris*, of which wound he dyed. In like case, may euery Statesman bee like *Achilles* in the generall body of his Actions, impassible and secure from any assault of wilfull and grosse ennor-

normitie : yet if he giue
way to *but one* handfull
(as it may be termed)of
Folly, not becomming
the grauity and greatnes
of his Calling; hee shall
soone meete with some
watchfull *Paris*, some
industrious Flatterer, or
ouer-busie enuious Cõ-
petitour, that will take
aduantage of his weak-
nesse, and wound his in-
firmitie to the ruine of
his Honours, if not to
the ieopardy of his life.

The period of all shal
be knit vp, with the ad-
uise of a famous learned
& Philosopher: & as he
wrote

wrote to his familiar
friend, let vs tranfcribe
to men in Authoritie;
Let a publike man re-
ioyce in the true pleafures
of a conftant Refolution,
not in the deceiuable
pleafures of vanitie and
fondneffe. By a good con-
fcience, honeft counfells,
and iuft actions, the true
good is acquired. Other
momentany delights only
fupple the forehead, not
vnburthen and folace the
heart. They are nothing,
alaffe they are nothing, it
is the minde muft be well
difpofed, it is the minde
muft bee confident : it is
the mind aboue all things

must be rectified; and the true comfort is not easily attayned, and yet with more difficulty retayned. But hee, he who directs all his whole priuate life in honourable proiections, cannot any way misse our L I N E O F L I F E, which points at the immortalitie of a vertuous name by profitably discharging the burthen of such imployments as are vsually imposed vpon those, whom their callings haue entitled *Publike men.*

A G o o d M a n is the last branch of *Reso-*

Of the 3 branch, A good Man.

solution, and by him is
meant (as is said before)
such a man, as doth (be-
side the care he hath of
himselfe in particular)
attend all his drifts and
actions, to bee a seruant
for others, for the good
of others, as if it were
his owne. School-boyes
newly trayned vp in the
Principles of Grammer
can resolue what a good
man is, or who ? Who ?
*Qui consulta patrum,
qui leges iuraq́; seruat.*
Such an one, as not in-
deed singly obserues
what he should doe, but
doth euen that which
hee

hee obserues hee should
doe. This man not only
liues, but liues well, re-
membring alwayes the
old adage ; that God is
the rewarder of Ad-
uerbes not of Nownes.
His intents are without
the hypocrisie of ap-
plause, his deedes with-
out the mercenary ex-
pectation of reward, the
issue of both is, all his
workes are crown'd in
themselues , and yet
crowne not him, for that
hee loues *Vertue* for it
selfe. *This man* neuer
flatters Folly in great-
nesse, but rather pitties,
and

and in pittie striues to
redresse the greatnesse
of Folly. *This man* ne-
uer enuies the eminence
of Authoritie , nor
feares the Enuious: His
reprehensiõs are balms,
his Prayses Glories, and
he is as thankfull to bee
rebuked, as to bee cheri-
shed. From such *a Man*
all things are to be grat-
fully accepted: His de-
sire to doe good to *all*,
hath not a like successe
to all (notwithstanding
in *him to will* is com-
mendable, and not to be
able *to doe*, pardonable.)
For it is not only the
pro-

propertie of true Ver-
tue , but also of true
Friendship, as well to
admonish, as to bee ad-
monished: For amongst
good men those things
are euer well taken that
are well meant; yet e-
uen *this man* (that vn-
compeld, vn-required,
not exacted, interposes
himselfe to set at vnitie
the disorders of others
not so inclinable to
goodnesse , is not free
from enmity, with those
whom in a general care,
he labours to deserue as
friends. The Reason,
Flattery procures frieds,
             Truth

Truth hatred. How? Truth Hatred? Yes, for from Truth is Hatred borne, which is the poyſon of Friendſhip, as *Lælius* wel obſerued: But what enſues? Hee whoſe eares are ſo fortified, and barrocaded againſt the admitment of Truth, that from his Friend he wil not heare the Truth, this mans ſafetie is deſperat: wherfore if any one will only reliſh *words of Downe and Honey*, as if wee loued to ſpeake nothing but *pure Roſes* (as the Prouerbe is:) let ſuch a one

Cicero de Amicit.

Plin. hift.
lib. 11. cap. 6

one learn from the skil-
full Artifts of Nature,
that the Bees doe an-
noint their Hiues with
the iuyce of the bitte-
reft Weeds, againft the
greedineffe of other
Beafts. Let him learne
from the skilfulleft Phi-
ficians, that the health-
fulleft Medicines fmart
moft in the Wound. Let
him learne from the

Arift. Eth.
lib. 3.

Prince of Philofophie,
that Anger was giuen to
men by Nature, (as hee
writes) as a Whetftone
of Valour; and then he
cãnot but confider, that
any paines which a *good*
(*Man*

Man vndergoes for reconciliation, be they either by way of admonition or reprehenſion, tend both to one end, that hee may make all like vnto himſelfe, that is, *Good Men*.

This very word (Good) implyes a deſcription in it ſelfe, more pithy, more patheticall, then by any familiar exemplification can bee made manifeſt: Such a man, as makes the generall commoditie, his particular benefit, may not vnfitly bee ſtiled a PRIVATE STATESꞁMAN:

MAN : His endeuours
are publike, the vſe pub-
like, the profit publike,
the commendation pub
like: But the perſon pri-
uate ; the Reſolution
priuate, the end priuate,
and the reward pecu-
liar.

It is impoſſible, that
the wretched and auari-
cious banking vp of
wealth , can draw him
into a conceipt, that hee
can euer make friends
of mony, after his death;
conſidering that the
World was created for
the vſe of men, and men
created into the World

to vfe it, not to enioy it.
This mans bounty is gi-
uing, not lending; and
his giuing, is free, not
referued: He cherifheth
Learning in the Lear-
ned, and incourageth
the Learned to the loue
of Learning by cherifh-
ing them; He heartneth
the vpright in Iuftice, &
ratifies Iuftice in the vpright; He helpes the di-
ftreffed with counfell,
and approoues the pro-
ceedings of wife Coun-
fellors. He is a patterne
to all what they fhould
bee, as to himfelfe what
he is.

Finally, try all his de-
fires, his actions are the
feafoners of his fpee-
ches, as his profeffion is
of his actions. Hee is a
Phyfitian to other mens
affections as to his own,
by comprimitting fuch
paffions as runne into
an infurrection , by
ftrengthening fuch as
decline , by fuppling
fuch as are inflamed,
by reftrayning fuch as
would runne out , by
purging fuch as ouer-
abound. His Ambition
climbes to none other
cure then to heale the
wounded, not to wound
the

the whole; beeing nei-
ther ſo vnwiſe to doe a-
ny thing that he ought
not to doe, nor ſo vn-
happy to doe any thing
what hee does not. His
ſingular misfortune is,
that (with *Druſus* an excellent man) he attempts
many times with a more
honeſt and good mind,
then good fortune and
ſucceſſe; inſomuch, as it
often comes to paſſe,
that other mens miſ-
chieſes are preferred be-
fore his Vertues: yet ſtill
as he is *a good Man*, iniu-
ries can no more diſ-
courage him, then ap-

Velleius biſt.Rom. lib.2.

F 3   plauſe

plauſe can ouer-weene
him.

Euen this man hath
his particular aduerſa-
ries to threaten him, and
(if it could be poſſible)
to terrifie him, and de-
ter him from the ſoli-
ditie of his temper:
Scandal to defame him,
and *impoſture* to tra-
duce him: *Flatterie and
enuie* are not a more pe-
ſtilent broode, ſet in
armes againſt a *publique
man*, then thoſe two
miſcreant monſters are
againſt a *good man*. But
is his reſolution any
way infracted, for that
ſome

some refractaries are (like Knights of the post) hired to witnesse against him? Doubtlesse no, but much the rather confirmed to run by a LINE OF LIFE, to the *Goale of Life*. His owne solace is to him, as an inexpugnable castle of strength, against all the forcible assaults of diuellish cóplots, built onely vpon this foundation, that he is conscious to himselfe of an vnforced sinceritie: With the Poet he can resolue: *Hic murus aheneus esto, nil conscire*

F 4

scire sibi, his integritie
to him is a Brazen wall;
And with the Orator,
he assures himselfe, that
nullum theatrum virtu-
ti maius conscientiâ,
Vertue hath not a more
illustrious and eminent
Theatre to act on, then
her owne conscience.
Socrates (a good man,
if a meere morrall man
may be termed so) bee-
ing scurrilously by *A-*
ristophanes the Poet,
derided before the
people ; and by *Any-*
tus and *Melytus* vn-
iustly accused before
the Iudges, as a trifler,
a ma-

Cicer. quæst.
Tusc. lib. 2.

In Comæd.
Νεφαλαις

Plat. apol.
Socrat.

a maſter of follies, a corrupter of youth, a ſower of impieties, anſwered; *If their alledged imputations be true, we will amend them; if falſe, they pertaine not to vs.* It was a noble conſtancie and reſolution of a wiſe man, that he (inlightned with the only beames of nature) was ſo moderate and diſcreet. The good man here perſonated (inſpired with a farre richer & diuiner knowledge then humanitie) cannot but aſmuch exceede *Socrates* in thoſe

Diog Laert, in vita Socrat.

F 5   ver-

vertues of resolution, as *Socrates* did his aduersaries in modestie and moderation.

Kings and mightie Monarches , as they are first mouers to all subordinate ministers, of what ranke or imploiments soeuer, within their proper dominions, are indeed *publike persons*; But as one king traffiques with another, another, and another, either for repressing of hostilitie , inlarging a confederacie , confirming an Amitie , setling a peace , supplanting

ting an heresie, and such
like, not immediately
concerning his owne
particular, or his peo-
ples; but for modera-
ting the differences be-
tweene other Princes:
In this respect euen
Kings and priuate men,
and so their actions be-
long wholly and onely
to themselues ; prin-
ting the royalty of their
goodnes, in an immor-
talitie of a vertuous and
euerlasting name , by
which they iustly lay a
claime to the Style *of
good men :* which at-
tribute doth more glo-
rifie

rifie their defert, then the mightineffe of their thrones can their glories.

In which refpect, our SOVERAIGNE LORD AND KING that now is, hath worthily chronicled his Grand-fathers remembrance, which was (as hee beft witneffeth) called *The poore mans King.* A title of fo ineftimable a wealth, that the riches of many Kingdomes are of too low & meane a value, to purchafe the dignitie and honour of this onely Style, *The poore*

Basiλ.
Δωρον.
lib.2.

poore mans King.

The famous and most excellent commendation of A Good Man, cannot be more expresly exemplified in any president or myrrour, by all the instances of former times, nor shall be euer (farre, farre bee seruilitie or insinuation) ouer-paralleled by any age succeeding, then in the person of I A M E S the King of great *Britaine* presently here reigning ouer vs. *A good man,* so well deseruing (from all gratefull memorie) seruice and

and honour, that not
to doe him seruice is an
ingratitude to the
*greatnesse of his good-
nesse* ; and not to doe
him all honour, an in-
gratitude to the *good-
nesse of his greatnesse.*
A good man, that euen
with his entrance to
the Crowne, did not
more bring *peace* to all
Christian nations, yea
almost to all Nations of
the Westerne World,
then since the whole
course of his glorious
reigne, hath preserued
peace amongst them. *A
Good man,* who hath
thus

thus long fought as an
equall and vpright mo-
deratour to decide, dif-
cuffe, conclude, and de-
termine all differences
between his neighbou-
ring Princes and fel-
lowes in Empire. *A
good man*, of whom it
may be verified that he
is Bonorvm Maxi-
mvs, and Magnorvm
Optimvs. *A good
man* , that loues not
vertue for the name of
vertue onely , but for
the fubftance and reali-
tie. *A good man*, whom
neither fcandal can any
way impeach of Iniu-
ftice,

ſtice, tyrannie, igno-
rance; nor impoſture
traduce, to a neglect of
merite in the deſertfull,
to leuitie in affections,
to ſurquedrie in paſſi-
ons, to intention of in-
clyning to folly, or
declyning from reall
worth; which as an he-
ditarie inheritance, and
a fee ſimple by nature
and education, hee re-
taynes in himſelfe, to
the wonder and admi-
ration of all, that may
emulouſly imitate him,
neuer perfectly equall
him. Queſtionleſſe,
the Chronicles, that
ſhall

shall hereafter report the Annalls of his life and Actions, shall doe infinite iniurie to the incomparable monuments of his name, if they Style him, as some would wish, IAMES THE GREAT, or as others indeuour, IAMES THE PEACEABLE, or as not a few hope, IAMES THE LEARNED. For to those titles haue the Greekes in *Alexander*, the Romans in *Augustus*, the Germans in *Charles the Fift*, the French men in *Charlemaine*, and

Henrie

Henrie the Fourth, Father to their prefent King, attayned : But if he fhall be reported in his *Style* to be, as in his owne worthineſſe hee may iuſtly challenge ; he muſt then be ſtyled, as by the approbation of all that truely know him, he is knowne to be IAMES THE GOOD. Let the ſumme of this branch of *Reſolution*, which is indeed *Corona operis*, the ſumme of the whole ſum , bee concluded : That *this onely patterne*, as he is onely inſerior on earth

to

to God, who is B o-
n v m S v m m v m, the
chiefe and soueraigne
good; so the distincti-
on betweene his great
Master and him (whose
Vicegerent he is) con-
sists in this (with reue-
rence to the diuine Ma-
iestie be it spoken) That
as God (whom to call
good is but an impro-
prietie of description)
is not singly *bonus*
good, but *Bonitas*
goodnesse, *in abstracto,*
(as the Schoole-men
speake:) So vnder the
great K i n g O f
K i n g s, this King of
men

men is substitute to his
King, with this vp·shut;
The one is foreuer the
King of goodnesse ; and
our King on earth, not
onely a *good King* , but
a *good man* ; Such a
good man as doth him-
selfe run, and teacheth
by his example, others
securely and readily to
runne, by his *Line of
Life*, to the immortali-
tie of a vertuous name.
A priuate man , *A
publique man* , *A good
man*, haue beene here
particularly deciphered
& discoursed. It comes
to conclusion, that hee,
           who

who defires either in his
owne perfon to be re-
nowned ; for the gene-
rall profperitie of the
Common-wealth, to be
eternized; or for the cō-
munitie of his friends,
or any whom hee will
make his friends, remē-
bred ; in the Diaries of
pofteritie, muft firft lay
the foundation of a wil-
lingneffe , from thence
proceed to a defire, frō
thēce to a delight, from
a delight to practife,
from practife to a con-
ftant perfeuerance in
noble actions. And then
fuch a man, howfoeuer,
he

he liue ſhall neuer miſſe
to end his dayes, before
his henors and the ho-
nours of his name can
end, for they ſhal know
no end; and yet euen in
death, and after death,
ouer-liue all his ene-
mies, in the immortall
ſpring of a moſt glori-
ous memorie ; which
is the moſt precious
Crowne and reward
of *A* moſt preci-
ous *Line of
Life.*

The

The Corollarie.

IN the view of the precedent Argument, somewhat (perhaps) too lamely hath the Progresse of a Mans Life (in any Fate) been traced; wherein still the course, like a Pilot sayling for his safetie and wel-fare, hath alwayes had an eie, to the North-Starre of Vertue: without which, men cannot but suffer shipwrack on the Land, aswell as Mariners on the Sea. Such as haue proofes in their

owne

owne perſons and ex-
periences of both for-
tunes, haue paſt through
their dangers of their
beeing MEN, as they
were firſt priuat; before
they entred : and from
their entrance waded,
into the Labyrinth of
Greatneſſe and Imploy-
ment, from whence they
becam *Publike mē.* Now
thē ſomwhat boldly (yet
the boldnes is a preſūp-
tion of loue, not loue of
preſumption) may bee
intimated ; that howſo-
euer, any great or po-
pular perſon, (for to
ſuch doth this applica-
tion

tion properly apper-
taine, howbeit free from
any particularity ex-
cept particularly chal-
lenged) in a peculiar
examination of himfelfe
cannot chufe, but find,
that he hath encountred
many Oppofitions of
Youth, (euen in graue
yeares) and frailtie (in
graue actions :) yet ha-
uing at any time, by any
cafualtie, a happineffe
(danger it felfe is a happineffe if rightly made
vfe of, otherwife a mife-
rie) to account with his
expence of time : hee
cannot vpon indifferent

G   and

and euen reckoning, in
ſtead of impayring his
Honours but aduance
them: he cannot, if hee
account faithfully, in-
ſtead of making the
World his Confeſſour,
but confeſſe his owne
Nobleneſſe; and there-
vpon He will find, that
the toyle in common af-
faires, is but traſh and
bondage, compared to
the ſweete repoſe of the
minde, and the good-
ly Contemplation of a
mans peace with Him-
ſelfe. All glory whether
it conſiſt of profits or
preferments, is WITH-
OVT

Ovt , and therefore makes nothing to the eſſence of true happineſſe : But the feeling of a reſolued conſtancie is Within, and euer keepes a Feaſt in a mans ſoundeſt content. One pregnant and notable Samplar deſerues an eye of Iudgement to be fixed on it. *Demoſthenes* after a long gouernment at his pleaſure in the Common-wealth (vpon what conſideration, He Himſelfe knew beſt, and Stateſ-men may eaſily gueſſe at,) is reported to confeſſe to his friends,

G 2   who

Plutarch.in vit.Demoſt.

who came to viſit him: That if at the Beginning *Two Waies* had bin propoſed before him ; *the one* leading to the Tribunall of Authoritie, *the other* to his Graue ; If Hee could by inſpiration, haue fore-knowne the Euils, the Terrors, the Calumnies, the Enuies, the Contentions, the Dangers, that men in ſuch places, muſt cuſtomarily meet with ; that Hee would much rather with alacritie, haue poſted on to his Sepulcher then to his Greatneſſe.

Brutus

Brutus when Hee deter-
mined his owne end,
cried out with *Hercules*:
O wretched and misera-
ble power of man , thou
wert nothing but a name,
yet I imbraced thee as a
glorious worke, but thou
wert a Bond-slaue to For-
tune.

It is superfluous to in-
large (or comment vp-
on) the Sufferings of
those famous Men : E-
uery mans owne talent
of Wisdome, and share
of tryall, may with not
much difficultie, conster
the sence of their mea-
nings. *A good Man* is

G 3   the

Dion. hist.
Rom. lib. 47.

the man, that euen the
greateſt or loweſt ſhould
both *bee*, and reſolue *to
be*. And this much may
be confidently auerred;
That men of eminent
commands, are not in
generall more feared in
the tyde of their great-
neſſe, then beloued, in
the ebbe of that great-
neſſe, if they beare it
with moderation. Sta-
tiſts honoured or fauou-
red, (for fauour and
honour are for the moſt
part inſeparable) haue
the eyes of the World
vpon their carriage, in
the carriage eyther of
their

their glories or deiecti-
ons : It is not to bee
doubted (which is a fin-
gular comfort) but any
fequeftration from a
woonted height, is only
but a tryall ; for beeing
managed with humble-
neffe and gratitude, it
may ennoble the Pati-
ents (for their owne par-
ticulars) to demeane
themfelues excellently,
in the places they had
before (may bee) fome-
what too neglectfully
difcharged. Alwayes
there is a Rule in obfer-
uation, pofitiue and me-
morable; that an inter-

position or ecclipse of
eminence, muſt not ſo
make a man vndervalue
his owne Deſert , but
that a *Noble Reſolution*,
ſhould ſtill vphold its
owne worth , in deſer-
uing well; if wee ayme
and intend to repute &
vſe Honours, but as in-
ſtrumentall cauſes of
vertuous effects in Acti-
ons. To all ſuch as ſo
doe, (and all ſhould ſo
doe that are worthy to
bee ſuch,) a ſeruice not
to be neglected is a pro-
per debt:eſpecially from
inferiour Miniſters to
thoſe, whoſe Creation,
hath

hath not more giuen them the prerogatiues of *being men*, then the vertuous *Resolution*, leading them by A LINE OF LIFE, hath adorned them, with the iust, knowne and glorious Titles of beeing *Good Men.*

VADVM *non transeat excors.*

FINIS.